THE

ART

OF

DRINKING SOBER

THE

ART

OF

DRINKING SOBER

50 Decadently Dry Cocktails
For All Occasions

MIRIAM NICE & RICHARD DAVIE

First published in Great Britain in 2020 by Seven Dials
an imprint of The Orion Publishing Group Ltd
Carmelite House, 50 Victoria Embankment
London EC4Y 0DZ

An Hachette UK Company

1 3 5 7 9 10 8 6 4 2

A CIP catalogue record for this book is
available from the British Library.
ISBN (Hardback) 978 1 8418 8427 1
ISBN (eBook) 978 1 8418 8428 8
Printed in China

MIX
Paper from
responsible sources
FSC® C008047

www.orionbooks.co.uk

CONTENTS

INTRODUCTION

A good cocktail isn't just a booze delivery system, it should be far more than the sum of its parts. Sharp-sweet fruit, fresh ice, hints of spice, fulsome bitterness and complex botanicals. Then there's the pleasing range of textures, be they smooth, frothy, effervescent, or viscous with cold. When you think about the cocktail experience, it's about so much more than a drink. There's the sense of occasion, the glassware, the garnishes, and the company you share it with. This was something we were very keen not to lose in reconsidering cocktails as an alcohol-free experience.

Approaching the recipes almost like a gustatory game of pick-up-sticks or Jenga, we wanted to remove the alcohol from some of our favourite cocktail recipes while leaving the structure standing unbowed.

We've used syrups, herbs, spices and vinegars to give support and build intensity, leaving the core profile of the cocktails otherwise intact. If you've enjoyed some of the original versions, you won't miss their alcoholic spine; and if you've never tried them, then this will give you access to some previously off-limits classics.

There's a certain amount of theatre in cocktails, so don't be tempted to scrimp just because there's no alcohol – you deserve a drink that's been taken seriously. While a sturdy jar will stand in, treat yourself to a decent shaker if you can. Don't skimp on the right glassware if you have it, and try to keep a surfeit of ice ready in the freezer.

ICE

Ice is vital in drinks-making, so don't treat it as an afterthought. It really is a key ingredient in its own right, giving you control over temperature and dilution. If you've got an event coming up, make up a decent surplus, as it disappears quickly. On a related note, try not to keep ice hanging around too long, as it will slowly pick up stale flavours from the other inhabitants of your freezer.

We'd recommend getting silicone trays, as the ease of turning out the ice cubes is liberating after the rigid plastic or metal trays of our youth. We have a couple of moulds that give us 2cm cubes, which suit us well for stirring, shaking and building up in the glass. When it comes to crushed ice, we recommend getting a smaller mould, ideally less than 1cm square or pea-sized. Novelty-shape trays are often quite good for this, as the ice cubes produced are usually fairly thin. The smaller size reduces the elbow grease required if you have a hand crusher, and also lessens the risk of damaging a blender, which is not unknown when breaking down bigger cubes. Lastly, if you see a good golf ball-sized mould, we find them excellent for slow sippers, as the lower surface area keeps them going for longer without watering down the drink unduly.

MEASURES

You'll also need measures – we use a double jigger that's 25ml one side and 50ml the other, but we also have a little 50ml glass one with 5ml increments (chef's measuring spoons fulfil the same purpose for dealing with fiddlier quantities). A good 500ml measuring jug from the kitchen will be useful, too, for the recipes involving larger quantities.

MIXING

For drinks where you're directed to stir, the ideal mixing set-up is a bar spoon and a mixing glass. Stirring down a drink involves simply mixing it with ice using a long-handled spoon until you're happy with how chilled and diluted it is. You can buy specialised mixing glasses – they're a bit like a heavier-duty pint glass but with a spout. If that seems an unwarranted expense, you can also use the main tin of a cocktail shaker or a measuring jug, as you prefer.

For shaken drinks, cocktail shakers are not all made equal. Try to find one you are comfortable with, and do practise a few times, even if just with water and ice, to get a feel for it. Miriam prefers a cobbler, the three-piece shaker most home bars use (a tin, a top with an inbuilt strainer and a small cap for the strainer), while Richard prefers shaker tins, which are an all-metal variant of the Boston shaker espoused by many professionals (a Boston consists of a reinforced pint glass and a larger tin, knocked together to form a seal and then shaken vigorously). Boston shakers, shaker tins and French/Parisian shakers have a slightly steeper learning curve than cobblers, but are simpler once you're used to them. A cobbler, however, doesn't require a separate strainer and is less likely to spray drink everywhere if you aren't paying attention.

If you're not very confident about using a cocktail shaker, we'd also recommend having a stick blender handy – they're so useful for getting the perfect foam on cocktails using egg white: ideal if you're as big a fan of a sour as we are.

STRAINERS

Most drinks will say to strain into the glass – this is so that you can hold back the ice, fruit and any other detritus to ensure the drink is in impeccable condition for its recipient. If you have a Boston, then this is done with a Hawthorne strainer, held to the lip of the tin, whereas a cobbler has the integral strainer. Where we say 'double-strain', we mean that you need to pass it through both this normal stage and then a second small sieve (a tea strainer is good), to remove any very fine pieces such as fruit pips or spices. Straining in two stages prevents larger ice shards and fruit pulp blocking the finer mesh of the second sieve.

Having laid down all these prescriptions, we should say one final thing: do not let a fear of doing things wrong get in the way of enjoying these drinks. Don't have a shaker? A Kilner jar will step in happily. Lack a sieve? Hold back what you can with a careful pour and judiciously placed fork – it'll still taste good!

We've loved creating these drinks and think there's something here for even the most special occasions. Whether you're hosting an event with all-alcohol-free drinks or just want one or two to punctuate the evening, there's something to please all tastes and seasons.

Cheers!

SYRUPS
&
INFUSIONS

'RUM' SYRUP

RHUBARB SYRUP

CASS-ISH

CHILLI INFUSION

GRAPE & CHAMOMILE WATER

'RUM' SYRUP

While we can't recreate the warmth that comes from being 40 per cent alcohol, we can at least give you the luxuriant body, dark sugar and spice of an aged dark rum with this syrup. With a splash of soda water, it tastes like a rum and cola; and the Hot Buttered Not Rum and Mock Mai-Tai build on that to delightful effect.

Makes: 250ml

INGREDIENTS:

120g dark brown muscovado sugar
2 teaspoons black treacle
100g fresh pineapple
200ml water
1 teaspoon black peppercorns
4 cloves
1 cinnamon stick
½ vanilla pod
1 strip of orange peel (cut with a vegetable peeler)

METHOD:

Put all of the ingredients in a saucepan and slowly bring to the boil. Cook for 2 minutes, then turn off the heat and leave to cool completely. Strain into a jug and keep in the fridge (will keep for up to a week).

Garnish/To Serve: ice and soda water, or use in Mock Mai-Tai (p. 125), Fruit Sangria (p. 116), Hot Buttered Not Rum (p. 108) and Dark & Stormy Soda (p. 111).

RHUBARB SYRUP

For the last few years, the Aperol Spritz and the Negroni have been inescapable delights — reviving interest in amari, *that broad Italian family of bitter, aromatic aperitifs. Here, then, is a syrup redolent of Campari, Aperol, Cynar or Zucca: fruity, tart, lightly bitter and oh-so-refreshing.*

Makes: 600ml

INGREDIENTS:

300g golden caster sugar
300ml water
1 orange, zest and juice (zest cut with a vegetable peeler)
1 red grapefruit, zest and juice (zest cut with a vegetable peeler)
400g rhubarb, chopped
1 small fresh beetroot, quartered

METHOD:

Put all of the ingredients in a large saucepan. Gently bring to the boil, then reduce to a gentle simmer until the rhubarb is really soft and breaking up.

Strain through a fine or muslin-lined sieve into a clean, heat-safe jug, then pour into a sterilised bottle. Seal and leave to cool, then store in the fridge for up to 2 weeks.

Garnish/To Serve: ice and tonic or soda water, or use in Grapefruit Spumoni (p. 26), Americano (p. 41), Tricyclette (p. 47), Rhubarb Spritz (p. 92) and Rhubarb Sour (p. 95).

CASS-ISH

Rich, intense and sweet, this is best served chilled with a splash of water on its own;
or to add a touch of luxury when added to fizzy business: either a sparkling wine,
or our own Kir Regal. Not half bad poured over good vanilla ice cream, either.

Makes: approx. 450ml

INGREDIENTS:

125g caster sugar
125ml water
1 bay leaf
3 black peppercorns
2 allspice berries
1 clove
250g frozen blackcurrants (or fresh when in season)
10ml balsamic vinegar
25ml lemon juice

METHOD:

Put the sugar, water, bay leaf, spices and blackcurrants in a pan. Heat gently until the sugar has dissolved and the mixture is simmering, stirring occasionally. Keep cooking until the blackcurrants have split and softened. Add the balsamic vinegar and lemon juice, then remove from the heat, allow to cool for 5 minutes and strain into a 500ml sterilised bottle. Keeps in the fridge for up to 1 week.

Garnish/To Serve: ice or a dash of water, or in Kir Regal (p. 71).

CHILLI INFUSION

The heat of chilli and the warmth of ginger are natural companions, especially
when complemented by the lime zest and coriander. With a fresh red twinge from
the chilli flesh, there's a sympathy to both rum and mezcal's flavour profiles.

Makes: 350ml

INGREDIENTS:

200g caster sugar
200ml water
1 slice fresh ginger
½–1 red chilli, sliced (adjust to taste)
1 lime, zest and juice
1 teaspoon coriander seeds

METHOD:

Put the sugar, water, ginger, chilli, lime zest and coriander seeds in a saucepan and
bring to the boil. Make sure the sugar has dissolved, then remove from the heat and
leave to cool. Strain into a jar or bottle and store it in the fridge for up to 2 days.

Serve in 25ml measures with the lime juice and a splash of soda.

Garnish/To Serve: as above, with ice, or in Pineapple Highball (p. 75), Palomita
(p. 84), Sherbet Margarita (p. 96) and Ginger Kicker (p. 122).

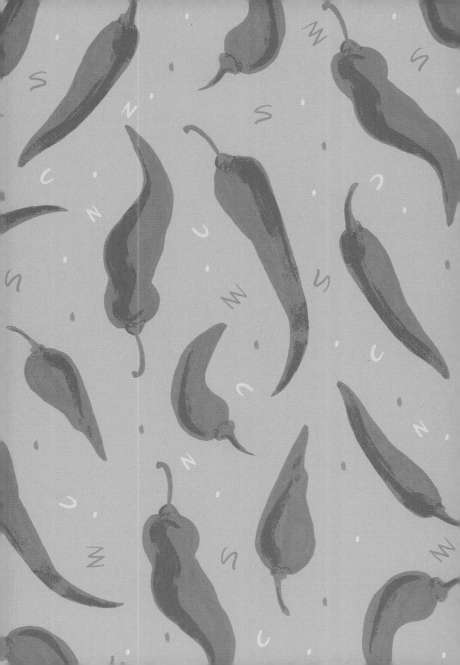

GRAPE & CHAMOMILE WATER

While it sounds very light from a quick perusal of the ingredients list, this is deceptively fulsome, the grapes and chamomile complementing each other to make a satisfying sipper for your wine glass or flute.

Makes: approx. 600ml

INGREDIENTS:

600ml water
1 teaspoon dried chamomile flowers
1 teaspoon coriander seeds
10 green grapes, halved
1 strip of lemon zest (cut with a vegetable peeler)
1 sprig of mint

METHOD:

Bring the water to the boil in a saucepan, take it off the heat then add the chamomile and coriander. Leave to cool, then add the grapes, lemon zest and mint. Transfer to a jug and chill for around 12 hours or up to 24 hours.

Strain into a jug and serve in white wine glasses in 125ml measures, or serve 100ml topped up with 75ml soda water like a white wine spritzer.

Garnish/To Serve: soda water. Optional – white grape juice, dash of elderflower cordial, sparkling water, or in Americano (p. 41).

BITTER
&
AROMATIC

GRAPEFRUIT SPUMONI

JUNIPER & TONIC

CUCUMBER SPRITZ

CARDAMOM SODA

ESPRESSO FAUX-TINI

HIBISCUS ICED TEA

DIRTY ROSEMARY-TINI

AMERICANO

ESPRESSO HIGHBALL

BREAKFAST SOUR

TRICYCLETTE

GRAPEFRUIT SPUMONI

*Our Rhubarb Syrup makes a stellar stand-in for amari like
Aperol or Campari in this zingy fruit refresher.*

Serves: 2

INGREDIENTS:

100ml Rhubarb Syrup (see p. 15)
100ml freshly squeezed red grapefruit juice
ice
150ml tonic water

METHOD:

Pour the rhubarb syrup and grapefruit juice into a jug along with a few cubes of ice.
Stir well until the outside of the jug feels really cold, then take out the ice. Now blitz
with a stick blender until the mixture is foamy. Divide between 2 highball glasses
and top with the tonic water. Garnish with a red grapefruit wedge.

Garnish/To Serve: 2 red grapefruit wedges.

JUNIPER & TONIC

A light alternative to the G&T, with the chamomile giving a touch of body to a refreshing long drink. Go heavy on the juniper if you want to lean into the gin notes.

Makes: 500ml juniper water

INGREDIENTS:

10g juniper berries
4 cloves
1 strip of lemon peel
pinch of dried chamomile flowers
500ml boiling water

METHOD:

Lightly crush the juniper berries with a pestle and mortar, just enough to crack the skin, then put them along with the cloves, lemon peel and chamomile flowers in a heatproof jug. Pour over the just-boiled water and leave to steep for 3 minutes. Strain, cool, then chill in the fridge.

Serve in 50ml measures over ice, with tonic water to taste. We like it 50ml juniper water, 100ml tonic and garnished with 3 more bruised juniper berries.

Garnish/To Serve: (per serving) 3 juniper berries, lightly bruised with a pestle and mortar.

CUCUMBER SPRITZ

Cucumber, it need hardly be said, is a summer refresher par excellence. *Given a lift with the delicate sweetness of fresh grapes, and nodding in the direction of the softer, cucumber-led gins of the last few years, this is one to pour into large glasses piled high with ice and enjoy on a bank holiday afternoon.*

Makes: 500ml infusion, 2 spritzes

INGREDIENTS:

for the cucumber infusion:

500ml cold water
½ cucumber, sliced
1 teaspoon coriander seeds
1 strip of lemon zest (cut with a vegetable peeler)
5 green grapes, cut in half
2 cloves
1 sprig of fresh mint

for the spritz:

ice
4 slices cucumber
2 mint leaves
100ml tonic water
100ml soda water

METHOD:

Start by making the infusion. Put all of the ingredients in a jug and steep in the fridge for 4 hours or overnight. Strain and discard all the ingredients from the drink. Will keep in the fridge for the rest of the day.

To make the spritz, fill 2 large copa de balon or red wine glasses with ice, garnish each with a couple of slices of cucumber and a mint leaf, then add 50ml of the infusion to each glass. Top both with 50ml tonic and 50ml soda and stir gently.

Garnish/To Serve: ice, cucumber slices, mint leaves.

CARDAMOM SODA

*Building on that mouthwatering cool/warm contrast in cardamom, with lime zest,
spices and the exceptional perfume rosewater always brings, this recalls some of the more
spicy gins currently on the market and is delightfully quick and easy to prepare.*

Makes: approx. 500ml infusion, 2 servings

INGREDIENTS:

for the cardamom infusion:

10g cardamom pods
4 cloves
1 strip of lime zest (cut with a vegetable peeler)
1 teaspoon coriander seeds
500ml boiling water

for the cocktail:

ice
1/2 teaspoon rosewater
150-200ml soda water or tonic water

METHOD:

Start by making the infusion. Lightly crush the cardamom pods with a pestle and
mortar, just enough to spilt the pod open, then put them in a heatproof jug along
with the cloves, lime zest and coriander seeds. Pour over the just-boiled water and
leave to steep for 3 minutes. Strain, cool, then chill in the fridge.

To make the cocktail, pour 50ml of the cardamom infusion into each of 2 copa de
balon or large red wine glasses. Fill up with ice, then add a few drops of rosewater
to each one and top with either soda or tonic water, or a mixture of both. Scatter in
a few cardamom pods to serve.

Garnish/To Serve: a few cardamom pods.

ESPRESSO FAUX-TINI

A non-alcoholic riff on that contemporary classic, the Espresso Martini, the balsamic vinegar gives a sharpness and richness that rounds it all out.

Serves: 4

INGREDIENTS:

for the coffee syrup:
100ml freshly brewed black coffee
10g light brown muscovado sugar
10ml maple syrup

for the cocktail:
150ml freshly brewed coffee, cooled
50ml balsamic vinegar
ice

METHOD:

Begin by making the coffee syrup. Mix the hot, strong black coffee with the muscovado sugar and maple syrup, stir until the sugar has dissolved, then leave to cool.

To make the cocktail, pour the coffee syrup, fresh coffee and the balsamic vinegar into a blender with a handful of ice. Blitz until frothy, then strain into 4 chilled martini glasses. Garnish each one with a coffee bean floating on the top.

Garnish/To Serve: 4 whole coffee beans.

HIBISCUS ICED TEA

The combination of hibiscus and Earl Grey alongside raspberries punches this up and gives a subtly different accent (and glorious colour) to this citrussy quencher.

Serves: 6

INGREDIENTS:

1 teaspoon dried hibiscus flowers or 1 hibiscus teabag
1 teaspoon Earl Grey leaf tea
80g fresh or frozen raspberries
1 tablespoon runny honey
1 litre boiling water
juice of 1 lemon
juice of 1 orange
ice

METHOD:

Put the hibiscus flowers, Earl Grey tea leaves, raspberries and honey into a large heatproof bowl or saucepan then pour over the boiling water. Leave to steep for 10 minutes, then strain into a large jug to cool completely. Add the lemon and orange juice. Stir in a few handfuls of ice, lemon slices and the leaves from 2 mint sprigs. Serve in tumblers with fresh ice and extra honey on the side.

Garnish/To Serve: 1 lemon, sliced; 2 sprigs of mint. Optional – ice, honey (to taste).

DIRTY ROSEMARY-TINI

Conceptually, this was the most difficult of the cocktails to envisage. Recreating as powerfully dry, punchy and subtle a cocktail as a Dirty Martini caused us no end of disagreement, but the chamomile and rosemary help add viscosity and aromatics that are redolent of the real thing. Don't skip the smoked salt: it's an essential bridge between the different flavour elements.

Makes: approx. 500ml

INGREDIENTS:

500ml water
1 strip of lemon peel (cut with a vegetable peeler)
pinch of dried chamomile flowers
4 sprigs of rosemary
5 cloves
8 crushed juniper berries
1 jar of green olives in brine
pinch of smoked salt

METHOD:

Bring the water to the boil, then drop in the lemon peel, chamomile, rosemary sprigs, cloves and juniper berries. Turn off the heat and leave to cool completely, then strain into a jug and chill in the fridge for at least 1 hour. At the same time, chill your martini glass(es).

To serve, pour 75ml of the rosemary mixture into a mixing glass or jug, add a large handful of ice and 3 teaspoons of brine from the jar of green olives. Stir the mixture until the outside of the jug feels very cold, almost too cold to touch. Strain into your chilled glass(es), stir in a pinch of smoked salt until dissolved and garnish with green olives on cocktail sticks.

Garnish/To Serve: ice, green olives, skewered on cocktail sticks (as many as you like).

AMERICANO

*Not quite the traditional aperitivo cocktail you're used to, but the rhubarb syrup
does a fine turn giving you that lip-smacking note Campari would normally impart.
Sip while dipping into that little bowl of plump olives and salted almonds.*

Serves: 1

INGREDIENTS:

25ml Rhubarb Syrup (see p. 15)
25ml white grape juice
25ml Grape & Chamomile Water (see p. 21, or you could use a non-alcoholic gin alternative)
ice
50ml tonic water

METHOD:

Pour the rhubarb syrup, grape juice and chamomile water into a tumbler with a few
ice cubes, stir gently, then top with chilled tonic water and garnish with a lemon slice.

Garnish/To Serve: 1 lemon slice.

ESPRESSO HIGHBALL

A touch left-field, this pairs best if you use a slightly lighter roast for your coffee, to emphasise the beans' green and fruity notes; but any which way, coffee, ginger and tonic deliver some intense refreshment.

Serves: 1

INGREDIENTS:

ice
75ml tonic water
75ml ginger beer
25ml freshly brewed espresso coffee, cooled

METHOD:

Fill a highball glass with ice, then add the tonic water and ginger beer. Stir just to combine, then slowly pour in the espresso coffee.

BREAKFAST SOUR

Like the Espresso Highball, this leans on the fact that coffee pairs remarkably well with other flavours, despite its sometimes bullish demeanour. Marmalade is a perfect vessel for orange's kinship with it, and given a little lift with egg white's effortless ability to make a cocktail better, this is a fine way to kick off a luxurious and celebratory Sunday brunch.

Serves: 4

INGREDIENTS:

for the marmalade syrup:

100ml water
50g marmalade
50ml espresso coffee
25ml cider vinegar

for the cocktail:

75ml lemon juice
75ml orange juice
ice
1 egg white

METHOD:

Start by making the syrup. Put the water and marmalade in a saucepan and bring to a simmer. Cook until the marmalade has dissolved, then leave to cool. Once cold, strain into a glass or cup and stir in the coffee and vinegar.

To make the cocktail, pour the syrup into a jug with the lemon and orange juice and add a good handful of ice. Stir the mixture until the outside of the jug feels cold, then strain out the ice. Add the egg white and pulse the mixture with a stick blender for a few seconds until frothed up. Pour the mixture into 4 ice-filled tumblers through a sieve. Garnish each one with a twist of orange zest and a coffee bean.

Garnish/To Serve: ice, 4 twists of orange zest and 4 coffee beans.

Tricyclette

The Bicyclette or Bicycletta is a delightfully simple aperitivo, *with a delightfully unverifiable rumour about the derivation of its name: elderly gents riding home rather wobbly after a few of these afternoon stiffeners. As this won't impair your roadworthiness, we thought it apposite to christen it the Tricyclette. Get home safe, everyone!*

Serves: 1

INGREDIENTS:

ice
50ml Rhubarb Syrup (see p. 15)
100ml white grape juice
1 teaspoon white wine vinegar

METHOD:

Fill a white wine glass with ice, then add the rhubarb syrup, grape juice and vinegar. Stir gently to combine, then garnish with a slice of lemon.

Garnish/To Serve: 1 lemon slice.

SWEET
& FRUITY

CUCUMBER DAIQUIRI

BLUEBERRY FIZZ

PIÑA COLADA SMOOTHIE

SHRUB COBBLER

PEACH JULEP

CITRUS COSMO

BUCKS FIZZ SODA

FRUIT CUP PUNCH

DRIVER'S SUNRISE

KIR REGAL

BRAMBLE (*SANS THORNS*)

PINEAPPLE HIGHBALL

CUCUMBER DAIQUIRI

*Made simply and with care, a daiquiri is a favourite cocktail of ours. Here,
cucumber's cooling qualities come to the fore in this tasty little short drink
that's ideal for when the weather passes from sultry to unbearable.*

Serves: 2

INGREDIENTS:

50ml lime juice
100ml cucumber infusion (see p. 30)
2 teaspoons agave syrup
1cm slice cucumber, cut into 4 pieces
ice

METHOD:

Pour the lime juice, cucumber infusion and agave syrup into a cocktail shaker. Add the cucumber pieces and a handful of ice. Shake until the outside of the shaker feels almost too cold to hold, then double-strain into 2 martini glasses. Garnish with a slice of cucumber perched on the rim of each glass.

Garnish/To Serve: 2 cucumber slices.

BLUEBERRY FIZZ

*The softness of blueberries meets the richness of coconut water in this
satisfying quencher. If anyone we knew had a lawn to play croquet on, then
a glass of this would be in my hand whenever a mallet wasn't.*

Serves: 2

INGREDIENTS:

50g blueberries
juice of 1 lemon
1 teaspoon granulated sugar
2 sprigs of mint
ice
50ml coconut water
100ml soda water

METHOD:

Put the blueberries, lemon juice and sugar in a large jug and press the mixture with
a cocktail muddler or the end of a bar spoon to lightly bruise all of the blueberries.
Pick the leaves from the mint sprigs and drop them into the jug too, along with a
generous handful of ice and the coconut water. Stir well to combine and dissolve
the sugar. Fill 2 tumblers with ice, then divide the blueberry mixture between them.
Top up with soda water and garnish with a few more blueberries.

Garnish/To Serve: ice, small handful of blueberries.

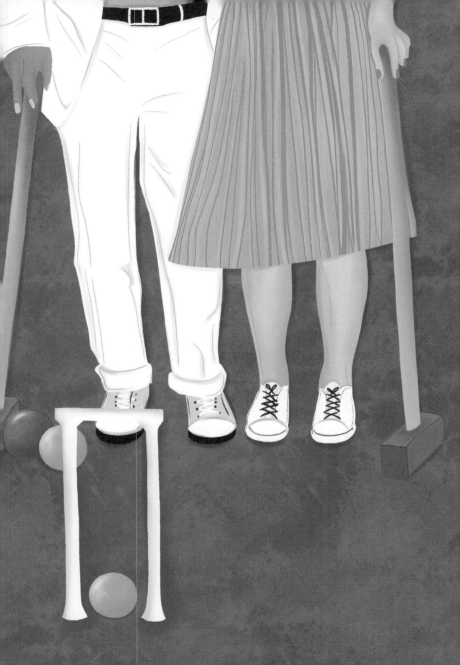

PIÑA COLADA SMOOTHIE

Coconut and pineapple are natural compatriots, and this alcohol-free riff on the iconic piña colada is well worth the extra step of spicing the rim, as it gives a little kick to every sip.

Serves: 2

INGREDIENTS:

300ml pineapple juice, chilled
100ml coconut milk
50ml lime juice
1 small banana, chopped
ice

for the spiced-lime sugar:

1 teaspoon cinnamon
zest of 1 lime, finely grated
½ teaspoon ground black pepper
½ teaspoon golden caster sugar
½ teaspoon runny honey

METHOD:

Start by making the spiced sugar. Put the cinnamon, lime zest, pepper and sugar on a saucer or small plate and stir together. Using a pastry brush, coat the rims of 2 hurricane glasses in a little honey, then dip them into the spice mix so it sticks. Now pour the pineapple juice, coconut milk, lime juice and banana into a blender. Blend until very smooth, then pour into the prepared glasses and add a few ice cubes and a cocktail cherry to garnish.

Garnish/To Serve: ice, 2 cocktail cherries, each skewered onto a cocktail stick.

SHRUB COBBLER

Shrubs are an undeservedly underappreciated family of drinks, and here they play a part in recreating another deeply underappreciated drink, the cobbler. Fruity but not sickly, this is a summery sipper that will appeal to any fans of sangria or Pimm's.

Serves: 6

INGREDIENTS:

2 oranges, diced into 1–2cm chunks (peel left on)
2 lemons, diced into 1–2cm chunks (peel left on)
100g pineapple chunks
50g runny honey
50ml sherry vinegar
ice
750ml soda water

METHOD:

Put half of the chopped fruit in a bowl and add the honey. Start to crush the fruit with a cocktail muddler, or what works best is a potato masher. Keep doing this until the pineapple has really broken up and you feel you've extracted as much juice as possible. Add the sherry vinegar and give it a really good stir. Sieve the mix into a large jug and add the remaining fruit pieces. Fill 6 tumblers with ice, then divide the fruit shrub mixture between them. Top with the soda water and stir gently just to fold the soda water into the mix. Garnish each one with a mint sprig and serve.

Garnish/To Serve: 6 sprigs of mint.

PEACH JULEP

We felt a little intimidated about toying with as fiercely held an institution as a julep at first, until we remembered that a lot of the old recipes involved a good whack of peach brandy alongside the bourbon. After that, it was a case of playing to the strengths of the luscious peach syrup, with perhaps a little nod to the familial resemblance the mojito and the julep share.

Serves: 6

INGREDIENTS:

100g golden caster sugar
50ml lemon juice
2 peaches, pitted and sliced
150ml white grape juice
ice
500ml soda water

METHOD:

Put the sugar, lemon juice and half the peach slices in a pan. Bring to the boil, then reduce the heat to a simmer and cook for around 3–4 minutes or until the peaches are soft and the sugar has dissolved. Leave to cool, then strain into a jug. Divide the peach syrup between 6 tumblers, then do the same with the remaining peach slices and grape juice. Add ice and stir, then top each one with some chilled soda water. Garnish with a mint leaf or two.

Garnish/To Serve: 2 sprigs of mint, leaves only.

CITRUS COSMO

While its star may have waned slightly since the heyday of Sex and the City, *the Cosmopolitan is still a fine little drink, especially if made with good ingredients. In that spirit, we started with actual cranberries and made the most of the fruit's affinity with oranges. Perfect for when you've got just the right new pair of shoes and want the world to know it.*

Serves: 4

INGREDIENTS:

for the cranberry infusion:

200g frozen cranberries
1 orange, zest and juice
2 tablespoons caster sugar
75ml water
2 cloves

for the cocktail:

juice of 1 lime
juice of 1 grapefruit
1 teaspoon orange marmalade
ice

METHOD:

Start by making the cranberry infusion. Put the cranberries, orange juice and zest, caster sugar, water and cloves in a saucepan and bring to the boil. Cook for about 5 minutes or until the cranberries are starting to soften. Remove from the heat and leave to cool. Strain and discard the cranberries.

To make the cocktail, pour the cranberry syrup into a large cocktail shaker, followed by the lime juice, grapefruit juice and marmalade, and then fill up with ice. Shake until the outside of the shaker feels very cold, then double-strain into 4 small martini glasses.

BUCKS FIZZ SODA

Although it might seem downright odd, using vinegar here gives you the acidity that makes many sparkling wines pop and brings in an alcohol-style prickle that really tricks the palate as you drink. Light, refreshing and rather more grown-up than you might imagine.

Serves: 2

INGREDIENTS:

100ml fresh orange juice
50ml pear juice
2 teaspoons white wine vinegar
150ml soda water

METHOD:

Make sure the juices and soda are all well chilled before you start. Divide the orange juice between 2 glasses. In a jug, combine the pear juice, vinegar and soda water, stir very briefly just to combine, then divide between the prepared glasses.

FRUIT CUP PUNCH

It's hard to imagine the grand British summer without at least dwelling for a moment upon a famous fruit cup. We couldn't persuade a particular well-known brand to knock us up a non-alcoholic batch, so we did the next best thing, which was to arrange this fruity little number.

Serves: 6

INGREDIENTS:

for the fruit infusion:

200g strawberries, chopped
1/2 cucumber, sliced
3 sprigs of mint
1 lemon, zest and juice
100g golden caster sugar
50ml water
4 cloves
1 cinnamon stick
25ml sherry vinegar

for the punch:

200g strawberries, sliced
4 sprigs of mint, leaves only
1/2 cucumber, sliced
1 orange, sliced
ice
750ml lemonade (clear, not cloudy)

METHOD:

Begin by making the fruit infusion. Put everything except the sherry vinegar in a saucepan and bring to the boil, stirring occasionally. Cook for 3-4 minutes or until the strawberries are soft and the sugar has dissolved. Take it off the heat and stir in the sherry vinegar. Discard the cinnamon stick and leave the mixture to cool and infuse. Once cold, strain and chill for 30 minutes.

To make the punch, pour the chilled infusion into a large jug or punch bowl. Add the punch ingredients and stir gently to combine. Serve in highball glasses.

DRIVER'S SUNRISE

When looking at the Tequila Sunrise, we felt it was vital to keep the iconic visuals. Lightly simmering only part of the orange juice with spices allowed us to give the drink that essential note of tequila complexity without leaving the drink tasting 'cooked'.

Serves: 4

INGREDIENTS:

500ml orange juice
8–10 white peppercorns
½ vanilla pod
1 teaspoon honey
1 teaspoon coriander seeds
2 teaspoons red wine vinegar
50ml grenadine

METHOD:

Pour half the orange juice into a saucepan, add the peppercorns, vanilla pod, honey and coriander seeds. Bring to a simmer, then turn the heat off and allow the mixture to infuse until completely cold. Once cold, stir in the remaining orange juice, then strain the mixture through a sieve into 4 ice-filled tall glasses. In a small jug, mix together the vinegar and grenadine, then slowly drizzle it on top of the juice in each glass – allowing it to slowly sink and create a rosy sunset effect. Add a cocktail cherry and a slice of fresh ginger to each glass to serve.

Garnish/To Serve: ice, 4 cocktail cherries, 4 slices fresh ginger.

KIR REGAL

The intensity of Cass-ish finds an ideal foil in this, which shares a few similarities with the Bucks Fizz Soda, where that prickle of acidity gives the drink a more grown-up air. Just the thing while the hors d'oeuvres are going round the room.

Serves: 2

INGREDIENTS:

50ml pear juice
2 teaspoons white wine vinegar
50ml soda water
2–4 teaspoons Cass-ish (see p. 16)

METHOD:

Make sure all the ingredients are thoroughly chilled first. Then, take 2 champagne flutes and pour 25ml pear juice and a teaspoon of vinegar into each one. Top with soda water, then slowly add 1–2 teaspoons of Cass-ish to each glass.

BRAMBLE (SANS THORNS)

Another modern classic, the Bramble is just the thing when autumn is peeking over the horizon but you don't quite want to let summer go. Precisely what you should reward yourself with after picking fruit and avoiding getting pricked.

Serves: 2

INGREDIENTS:

crushed ice
50ml lemon juice
100ml juniper water (see p. 29), or use a non-alcoholic gin alternative
2 teaspoons runny honey
70g fresh blackberries
25ml sherry vinegar
ice

METHOD:

Fill 2 tumblers with crushed ice. Then pour the lemon juice, juniper water, honey, blackberries and sherry vinegar into a cocktail shaker with a handful of ice cubes. Shake hard, then double-strain this slowly into the glasses over the crushed ice. Garnish with a few extra whole blackberries.

Garnish/To Serve: a few fresh blackberries.

PINEAPPLE HIGHBALL

*The intensity of flavour and acidity that you get with pineapple seemed like
a match made in heaven with the heat and sweet/savoury prickle of the
chilli syrup, and so it proved to be. Hawaiian shirt not required.*

Serves: 1

INGREDIENTS:

25ml Chilli Infusion (see p. 18)
50ml pineapple juice
100ml soda water
ice

METHOD:

Combine all the ingredients together in a highball glass with lots of ice. Garnish
with a mint sprig and a wedge of fresh pineapple.

Garnish/To Serve: 1 sprig of mint, 1 fresh pineapple wedge.

SOUR

APPLE & RASPBERRY SPRITZER

LIME COOLER

PALOMITA

DOUBLE MINT MOJITO

MARZIPAN SOUR

GRAPEFRUIT COOLER

RHUBARB SPRITZ

RHUBARB SOUR

SHERBET MARGARITA

LAPSANG SOUR

GIM-LESS

EARL GREY SOUR

APPLE & RASPBERRY SPRITZER

Simple, pleasing and, if you have some fruit in the freezer, a cinch to put together. As with a lot of these drinks, the touch of vinegar gives both depth and structure while adding a slightly 'grown-up' note.

Serves: 1

INGREDIENTS:

25ml apple juice
1 teaspoon apple cider vinegar
handful of fresh or frozen raspberries
100ml soda water
ice

METHOD:

Combine all of the ingredients together over ice in a white wine glass. Stir gently to mix, then add a sprig of dill to garnish.

Garnish/To Serve: 1 sprig of dill.

LIME COOLER

You put the lime in the coconut, as Harry Nilsson once sang. While he was most unlikely to have stopped there, we have, as this is a glorious melding of flavours and the coconut water again adds body to this tropical pleaser.

Serves: 1

INGREDIENTS:

50ml fresh lime juice
2–3 lime slices
ice
100ml coconut water
100ml soda water

METHOD:

Pour the lime juice into a highball glass with the lime slices, ice and coconut water. Stir gently to combine, then add the soda water and stir once more.

PALOMITA

*We're quietly rather proud of this chilli syrup, as it inveigles its way happily into
drinks that would use rum or tequila. Here, it does a sterling job of replicating tequila
in a long drink that got one of our tasters quite merry, despite the lack of alcohol.
Mission accomplished, we felt, and so this little sibling to the Paloma was born.*

Serves: 1

INGREDIENTS:

ice
25ml Chilli Infusion (see p. 18)
25ml lime juice
50ml grapefruit juice
100ml soda water

METHOD:

Put a teaspoon of flaky salt on a small plate or saucer, dip a tumbler in a little water
then into the salt to coat the rim of the glass. Then add a handful of ice, the chilli
infusion, lime juice, grapefruit juice and soda water. Stir gently to combine and
garnish with a wedge of grapefruit.

Garnish/To Serve: flaky sea salt (smoked sea salt if you can get it), grapefruit wedge.

DOUBLE MINT MOJITO

*Mint, lime and sugar are such a natural combination that you won't
miss the rum. Delightfully refreshing, sip it through a straw as you
consider slipping back into the water on a scorching day.*

Serves: 1

INGREDIENTS:

juice of 1 lime
½ teaspoon sugar
1 sprig of mint, leaves only
ice
75ml brewed and cooled mint tea (made from leaves or a mint teabag)
100ml soda water

METHOD:

Put the lime juice, sugar and mint leaves in the bottom of a highball glass, and crush
lightly with a cocktail muddler or the end of a wooden spoon. Add a good handful
of ice, then pour over the cooled mint tea. Stir carefully so as not to bruise the mint
too much, then top with soda water.

MARZIPAN SOUR

For all the sours in this book, we've used a stick blender as it gives quick and reliable results, but you can do this in a cocktail shaker if you prefer. If so, a 'reverse dry shake' is our preferred method (shake everything but the egg white with ice; remove ice and add egg white; shake again hard; serve) for flavour, froth and dilution.

Serves: 4

INGREDIENTS:

for the marzipan syrup:

100ml water
150g golden caster sugar
4 prunes
pinch of ground cinnamon
1 teaspoon almond extract

for the cocktail:

150ml lemon juice
ice
1 egg white

METHOD:

Start by making the syrup. Put the water, sugar, prunes and cinnamon in a saucepan and bring to a simmer. Cook until the sugar has dissolved, then leave to cool. Once cold, discard the prunes and add the almond extract.

To make the cocktail, pour the marzipan syrup into a jug with the lemon juice and a good handful of ice. Stir the mixture until the outside of the jug feels cold, then strain out the ice. Add the egg white and pulse the mixture with a stick blender for a few seconds until frothed up. Pour the mixture into 4 ice-filled tumblers through a sieve. Garnish with a maraschino cherry on a cocktail stick.

Garnish/To Serve: ice and 4 maraschino cherries, each skewered on a cocktail stick.

GRAPEFRUIT COOLER

Simple, but the reduction of some of the grapefruit juice gives this one a hitting power beyond its ingredients list. A most pleasing way to start the evening as winter finally gives way to spring.

Serves: 2

INGREDIENTS:

150ml grapefruit juice
ice
200ml soda water

METHOD:

Pour 50ml of the grapefruit juice in a saucepan and simmer until it reduces by half. Leave to cool, then combine with the remaining grapefruit juice. Fill 2 highball glasses with ice, then divide the grapefruit mixture between them. Top with soda water and garnish with Thai basil.

Garnish/To Serve: 2 sprigs of Thai basil.

· BARBADOS ·

PLATINUM COAST

St Nicholas Abbey

Gibbes Beach

Flower Forest

Martin's Bay

Holetown

George Washington House

Bottom Bay

Carlisle Bay

Oistin Bay

Sliver Sands Beach

RHUBARB SPRITZ

Like the Grapefruit Spumoni, this really shows the rhubarb syrup off to best effect. With spritzes more popular than they've been in a long time, here's an alternative you can be happy to be seen with.

Serves: 1

INGREDIENTS:

ice
50ml Rhubarb Syrup (see p. 15)
25ml lemon juice
25ml white grape juice
10ml white wine vinegar
100ml soda water

METHOD:

Put a generous handful of ice in a large wine glass. Pour in all the rest of the ingredients and stir briefly to combine. Garnish with an orange wedge and a sprig of fresh basil.

Garnish/To Serve: 1 orange wedge, 1 sprig of basil.

RHUBARB SOUR

It's so pink! Take advantage of egg white's miraculous ability to soften and enrich flavours and whip up some of these mouthwateringly juicy little numbers.

Serves: 4

INGREDIENTS:

250ml Rhubarb Syrup (see p. 15)
150ml lemon juice
½ teaspoon vanilla essence
ice
1 egg white

METHOD:

Pour the syrup into a jug with the lemon juice and vanilla essence, then add a large handful of ice. Stir the mixture until the outside of the jug feels cold, then remove the ice cubes with a spoon and discard. Add the egg white and pulse the mixture with a stick blender for 5–10 seconds until it froths. Divide the mixture between 4 tumblers with a few cubes of fresh ice. Garnish each one with a ribbon of fresh rhubarb.

Garnish/To Serve: ice, ½ stick rhubarb – cut 4 ribbons from it, using a vegetable peeler.

SHERBET MARGARITA

Again, the chilli syrup plays a blinder, standing in for tequila in this pleasingly ridiculous little number. Do take the time to sherbet the rims as that initial zing is all part of the fun.

Serves: 2

INGREDIENTS:

1 lime wedge
1 teaspoon sherbet from a dipper sachet
50ml Chilli Infusion (see p. 18)
50ml lime juice
1 teaspoon marmalade
1 teaspoon white wine vinegar
pinch of black pepper
pinch of ground coriander
1/2 teaspoon vanilla extract
ice

METHOD:

Run the lime wedge around the rims of 2 margarita glasses or tumblers. Pour the sherbet powder onto a small plate or saucer, then dip the glasses into it to coat the rims in the sherbet.

Put the rest of the ingredients into a cocktail shaker with a generous handful of ice. Shake until the outside of the shaker feels very cold. Fill the prepared glasses with crushed ice, then double-strain the cocktail over the top.

Garnish/To Serve: crushed ice.

LAPSANG SOUR

Lapsang Souchong's smoky air may be slightly divisive among tea drinkers, but here it gives you another dimension in this perfect pre-prandial number.

Serves: 4

INGREDIENTS

250ml freshly brewed Lapsang Souchong tea, cooled
1 tablespoon marmalade
75ml orange juice
75ml lemon juice
30ml sugar syrup
ice
1 egg white

METHOD:

Pour the tea and marmalade into a jug with the fruit juices and sugar syrup, then add a large handful of ice. Stir the mixture until the outside of the jug feels cold, then remove the ice cubes with a spoon and discard. Add the egg white and pulse the mixture with a stick blender for 5–10 seconds until it froths. Divide the mixture between 4 tumblers with a few cubes of fresh ice. Garnish each one with a black cherry or a twist of lemon zest.

Garnish/To Serve: ice, 4 black cherries (fresh or preserved) or 4 twists of lemon zest.

GIM-LESS

A gimlet sans *gin? Why not?! The cordial is key here, so do take the time to make it yourself, as that's where you're going to get much of this drink's lift. With that in mind, stir it down thoroughly unless you like your drinks sweeter.*

Serves: 1

INGREDIENTS:

for the cordial:

1 lime, zest and juice
1 lemon, zest and juice
25ml water
150g caster sugar

for the cocktail:

50ml cardamom infusion (see p. 32) or another non-alcoholic gin alternative
ice

METHOD:

Begin by making the cordial. Put the lime zest and juice along with the lemon zest and juice into a saucepan. Add the water and sugar. Heat gently until the sugar has dissolved and the mixture is beginning to simmer. Turn off the heat and leave to cool before straining.

To make the cocktail, pour 50ml of the strained syrup into a mixing glass or jug and add the cardamom infusion and a good handful of ice. Stir until the outside of the glass feels really cold, almost too cold to handle, then strain into a coupe glass. Garnish with a lime slice or in the summer a fresh organic rose petal.

Garnish/To Serve: lime slice or rose petal.

EARL GREY SOUR

Of all the sours in this book, this tastes the least directly like its title. While that might appear an odd way to lead into the recipe, what we want to highlight is that this one might surprise you, with its layered citrus ingredients and slight touch of dryness. A sour for the summer?

Serves: 4

INGREDIENTS:

200ml freshly brewed Earl Grey tea, cooled
50ml cardamom infusion (see p. 32) for other non-alcoholic gin alternative
150ml lemon juice
2 teaspoons lemon curd
ice
1 egg white

METHOD:

Pour the tea and cardamom infusion into a jug with the lemon juice and lemon curd, then add a large handful of ice. Stir the mixture until the outside of the jug feels cold, then remove the ice cubes with a spoon and discard. Add the egg white and pulse the mixture with a stick blender for 5–10 seconds until it froths. Divide the mixture between 4 tumblers with a few cubes of fresh ice. Garnish each one with a piece of crystallised ginger and a twist of lemon zest threaded onto a cocktail stick.

Garnish/To Serve: ice, 4 strips of lemon zest, 4 cubes of crystallised ginger, 4 cocktail sticks.

SPICED
& SMOKY

HOT BUTTERED NOT RUM

DARK & STORMY SODA

MULLED 'WINE'

MULLED APPLE JUICE

FRUIT SANGRIA

VIRGIN MARY

SHANDYGAFF

GINGER KICKER

MOCK MAI-TAI

NEW NEW YORK SOUR

HOT BUTTERED NOT RUM

Hot buttered rum, in its original form, is one of Richard's favourite winter drinks.
While putting butter into a hot drink may seem strange (and without alcohol to act
as an emulsifier, the cinnamon stick is needed to give an occasional stir, as well as to
bring flavour), this is a pleasingly unctuous warmer for those long, cold nights.

Serves: 2

INGREDIENTS:

15g butter
1 cinnamon stick
1 slice fresh ginger
50ml 'Rum' Syrup (from p. 12)
100ml water

METHOD:

Put all of the ingredients in a saucepan and heat gently until the butter has melted
and the mixture starts simmering. Pour into 2 small heatproof glasses or teacups
to serve, leaving the ginger and cinnamon stick behind. Serve with fresh cinnamon
sticks to use as stirrers.

Garnish/To Serve: 2 cinnamon sticks.

DARK & STORMY SODA

A simple highball classic, we found that our 'Rum' Syrup was sweet enough to give this soda/ginger mix a good balance of flavours, the ginger beer pepping up the rich, dark sugar and spice of the syrup.

Serves: 1

INGREDIENTS:

ice
25ml lime juice
50ml soda water
50ml ginger beer
35ml 'Rum' Syrup (from p. 12)

METHOD:

Fill a highball glass with plenty of ice. Add the lime juice, soda and ginger beer and stir gently to combine. Slowly pour in the 'rum' syrup, then garnish with a bushy sprig of thyme as a stirrer.

Garnish/To Serve: 1 sprig of thyme.

MULLED 'WINE'

A traditional mulled wine is all too often an excuse to smother cheap plonk in spices and punch it up with brandy. Here, we've bolstered the obvious grape juice with some of pomegranate's zing, complexity and tannins from soft fruit and a wider range of spices for something to see you through autumn nights.

Serves: 4–6

INGREDIENTS:

250ml red grape juice
250ml pomegranate juice
100g frozen mixed berries
1 cinnamon stick
1 clementine (or other small orange), sliced
5 cloves
5 black peppercorns
1 tablespoon golden caster sugar
1 teaspoon coriander seeds
1 slice fresh ginger

METHOD:

Put all of the ingredients together in a saucepan and heat gently until the sugar has dissolved and the mixture is simmering. Reduce the heat and continue to warm for 5 minutes before straining into heatproof glasses or teacups.

MULLED APPLE JUICE

Mulled cider has always languished in the shadow of mulled wine, very unfairly in our opinion, so this was a chance to right that wrong. A few savoury notes add a whole lot to this, so don't look askance at the sage, thyme and rosemary.

Serves: 4

INGREDIENTS:

500ml cloudy apple juice
1 lemon, cut into quarters
2 sage leaves
1 sprig of thyme
1 sprig of rosemary
1 cinnamon stick
4 cloves
1 teaspoon honey
1 teaspoon cardamom pods

METHOD:

Put everything together in a saucepan and heat gently until the honey has dissolved and the mixture starts to simmer. Turn the heat down and continue to cook gently for 5 minutes before straining into heatproof glasses or teacups.

Garnish/To Serve: 4 sprigs of thyme or rosemary, or a mixture.

FRUIT SANGRIA

*The 'Rum' Syrup does sterling service here, adding a spicy bottom note in
the absence of a hearty table wine. Bolstered with all manner of fruit, this
is exactly what you want in midsummer when it's too hot to eat early, and
a glass of something helps while away the evening with family.*

Serves: 8

INGREDIENTS:

500ml red grape juice
250ml white grape juice
25ml 'Rum' Syrup (see p. 12)
1 orange, chopped
1 lemon, chopped
1 nectarine, pitted and chopped
1 green apple, chopped
handful of strawberries, hulled and halved
a few fresh cherries, pitted and halved
ice
250ml tonic water

METHOD:

Put all of the ingredients except the ice and tonic water into a large jug or punch
bowl and stir. Leave to infuse in the fridge for at least 20 minutes or up to an hour,
then add the ice and tonic water. Stir gently to combine and serve.

VIRGIN MARY

Playing around with the tomato-juice base gives this riff on the Bloody Mary, with grape juice adding a touch of sweetness and sherry vinegar a bit of fight to this Saturday brunch standby.

Serves: 2

INGREDIENTS:

400ml tomato juice
100ml red grape juice
juiced of ½ lemon
10ml sherry vinegar
ice
½ teaspoon Worcestershire sauce
4 dashes Tabasco
pinch of ground black pepper
pinch of celery salt

METHOD:

Pour the tomato juice, grape juice, lemon juice and vinegar into a jug and add a handful of ice. Add the Worcestershire sauce, hot sauce, black pepper and celery salt and stir again. Divide between 2 ice-filled tall glasses and add a celery stick and lemon wedge to each glass

Garnish/To Serve: ice, 2 sticks of celery, 2 lemon wedges.

SHANDYGAFF

*Richard has always been a fan of a bitter/ginger beer shandy, so this seemed a no-brainer.
The only thing we'd say is that one of the new wave of low-alcohol pale ales would be a good
place to start, as some low-alcohol lagers are too light to stand up against a proper ginger
beer. Current brands by Adnams, Thornbridge and Big Drop are all solid options.*

Serves: 4

INGREDIENTS:

ice
250ml no-alcohol beer
250ml ginger beer

METHOD:

Fill 4 half-pint glasses with ice, then gently pour in the beer followed by the ginger
beer. Stir gently to combine.

GINGER KICKER

*Smoky tea is just the thing to buttress ginger beer without oversweetening things,
as the chilli infusion makes another appearance. With lime shaping everything
up, this is a great accompaniment to the smoke and char of barbecue food.*

Serves: 4

INGREDIENTS:

100ml freshly brewed Lapsang Souchong tea, cooled
200ml ginger beer
100ml Chilli Infusion (from p. 18)
150ml lime juice

METHOD:

Pour the tea, ginger beer, chilli infusion and lime juice into a jug and stir well to
combine. Fill 4 tall glasses with ice, then pour the cocktail over the top. Stir each
one briefly and garnish with lime, coriander and chilli.

Garnish/To Serve: ice, 4 lime wedges, 4 sprigs of fresh coriander, 4 small red chillies.

MOCK MAI-TAI

*While using almond essence in place of an orgeat syrup feels a bit like cheating,
it keeps things quick and snazzy in this tribute to a tiki drink legend.*

Serves: 1

INGREDIENTS:

25ml 'Rum' Syrup (from p. 12)
a few drops of almond extract
1 teaspoon marmalade
½ teaspoon cider vinegar
25ml pomegranate juice
25ml lime juice
ice

METHOD:

Combine all the ingredients in a mixing glass with ice, then double-strain into a
tumbler over fresh ice, taste and add a splash of water if too sweet. Garnish with a
couple of maraschino cherries threaded onto a cocktail stick.

Garnish/To Serve: 2 maraschino cherries.

NEW NEW YORK SOUR

A visual pleasure as much as anything, with that layer of red floating daintily under the foam and over the rest of the cocktail, this was a joint favourite of us both. Give yourself time to not only pour the grape juice float, but also to let it settle in the right place – it will happen!

Serves: 4

INGREDIENTS:

for the syrup:

100g golden caster sugar
200ml water
1 orange, peel cut in long strips with a vegetable peeler
1 sprig of fresh rosemary

for the cocktail:

100ml freshly brewed Lapsang Souchong tea, cooled
100ml lemon juice
ice
1 egg white
75ml red grape juice

METHOD:

To make the syrup, put all the ingredients into a saucepan, bring to the boil, then remove from the heat and allow to cool. Discard the orange peel and rosemary.

Pour the syrup into a jug and add the tea and lemon juice and add a handful of ice. Stir until the outside of the jug feels really cold, then discard the ice and add the egg white. Pulse the mixture with a stick blender until the egg white is frothy, with fine bubbles and starting to increase in volume. Fill 4 tumblers with ice, then divide the cocktail mixture between them. Divide the grape juice between the glasses, adding it very slowly (pouring carefully over the back of a teaspoon helps) so that it gently floats on top of the drink but just under the egg white. Let the drinks settle for a moment before serving.

Garnish/To Serve: ice.

HUDSON RIVER
Central Park
Broadway
Empire State
Chrysler
Chelsea
TAXI
NYC
Flatiron
Soho
Financial district
Brooklyn
Liberty Island
·NEW YORK·

INDEX

ACKNOWLEDGEMENTS

We would like to thank our family and friends for their unstinting support in this endeavour. Special note should be made of Samuel Kirk and Kristina Spindler, who each came over and helped us power through so very, very many recipes.

ABOUT THE AUTHORS

MIRIAM NICE and RICHARD DAVIE are both food and drinks writers. Miriam works for BBC Good Food and Richard is a freelance drinks writer. Miriam is a recipe writer, presenter and illustrator and loves a culinary challenge. Richard is a trained brewer and also works at award-winning micro pub The Beer Shop. They live in South London.

KATY ALCOCK is a freelance illustrator with a keen eye for beautiful colour combinations and sources inspired from the world around us. She shares her work through her Instagram account @simply_katy and sells her prints through Etsy (SimplyKatyPrints).